THE OFFICIAL SINKIES DON'T COOK BOOK

Norm Hankoff

FRESS PRESS

Edited by Bruce Robinson
Illustrated by Larry Bulawsky

Fress Press

SINKIE World Headquarters
N.H. ASSOCIATES
1579 Farmers Lane, #252
Santa Rosa, California USA 95405

ISBN 0-9637354-0-3

Library of Congress Catalog Card Number: 93-72150

Printed in The United States of America

"...First there were foodies, now there are Sinkies..."
– Los Angeles Times

"...It's safe to say we've all been guilty of it at least once in our lives..."
– *Santa Rosa Sun*

"...It's a great idea...calories disappear when they slide down your elbow and go into the drain..."
– *Syndicated Columnist Erma Bombeck*

"...Good luck from a fellow Sinkie...and don't put celery in the disposal..."
– *Herb Caen, San Francisco Chronicle*

"...Too busy to hassle with the formalities of place settings? You're not alone. There's even a club for people like you..."
– *Entrepreneur Magazine*

"...Self-help group for those addicted to faucet chow..."
– *Sonoma County Business Magazine*

"...One of the largest and most neglected culinary groups finally has an identity..."
– *Chicago Tribune*

"...Up, up with Sinkies!...Sinkies stand tall..."
– *New York Daily News*

"...I, too, have eaten many a meal over the sink...
– *Mike Nichols, Fort Worth Star-Telegram*

"...Sinkies...attracting considerable attention..."
– *Gaye LeBaron, Santa Rosa Press Democrat*

"...We all have known times when the kitchen sink has a unique appeal for speed and efficiency...
– *Syndicated Columnist Susan Deitz, Single File*

"...For What It's Worth: This is to be sure you've heard about the Sinkies, in case you're eligible for membership..."
– *Paul Harvey, ABC Radio Network*

"...Get your incredibly classy Sinkie certificate..."
– *Sonoma County Style Magazine*

"...Table (Sink) for one, Sir?..."
– *Dayton Daily News*

"...I've been eating over the kitchen sink all my life..."
– *Ray Orrock,*
San Francisco Bay Area Alameda Newspaper Group

"...Sinkies stand up for their bites..."
– George Hower, Santa Rosa Press Democrat

"...Have I got the perfect club for you to join...The Sinkie Association for short. Sinkies for shorter..."
– Jann Malone, Richmond Times-Dispatch

"...Thanks for the membership certificate. Unfortunately, I got tomato sauce all over it..."
– Syndicated Columnist Dave Barry

"..Dining with pleasure, over the sink...."
– Sarasota Herald-Tribune

"...Sinkies unite for their official cookbook..."
– Portland Oregonian

"...What distinguishes Sinkies? Seeing things in a different light..."
– Arizona Republic

"Eating over the sink can earn you an award..."
– Omaha World Herald

"..He also dines who dines over the sink.."
– Greensboro News & Record

"...Over-the-sink diners spout group identity..."
– Boulder Daily Camera

"...Another kind of food club takes shape..."
– Milwaukee Journal

"...Ever feel you're on the brink? Just eat over the kitchen sink..."
– Salt Lake Tribune

THE
OFFICIAL
SINKIES
DON'T COOK BOOK

This Don't Cook Book is dedicated to Sinkies everywhere. The few who admit it and the many who don't. To them we say, be proud. Hold your heads up high. Not too high. Crumbs, drips and dribbles happen.

TABLE OF CONTENTS

This book has none.
Most Sinkies don't bother much with tables.

HOW
THE SINKIE ASSOCIATION
BEGAN

Late one afternoon in 1991, Norm Hankoff was standing at his kitchen sink, scarfing down some tuna salad, using extra-strength, corrugated potato chips as utensils.

Inexplicably, something compelled him to raise his eyes in mid-chew. There, just above his head, he saw what he clearly knew to be a light bulb. But THIS light bulb was not connected to anything, yet it was definitely on and burning brightly.

As he stood there puzzled, squinting at the light, directly above it appeared the letters S I N K I E. At that instant, what he saw finally made sense. Hankoff, and millions of others around the world, had, for hundreds of years, been "SINKIES" without realizing it. He squinted again above the bulb just long enough to envision adding the tiny letters "™." Next, he jotted down a few notes about this noteworthy experience and immediately added a little circle, inside of which he placed the tiny letter "c." "One cannot be too careful, can one?" he thought. Then, he turned on the cold water faucet and the garbage disposal and "Poof!" the light bulb disappeared.

Hankoff knew he had been present at the birth of a nice little cottage industry which someday would become big enough to do worthwhile things for deserving people.

From this extraordinary beginning, Norm Hankoff decided to dedicate a significant portion of the rest of his life to the betterment of SINKIEKIND, while causing his children and grandchildren as little embarrassment as possible.

FOREWORD TO THE PREFACE TO THE INTRODUCTION

Ever since it became known to the world that this book was in the planning stages, the reaction has been nothing short of extraordinary. Enthusiastic Sinkies from all over the map have expressed their fervent desire to have the book available as soon as possible, as in yesterday. It's not surprising they would be an impatient lot; it is the essential nature of a Sinkie to place great value on life's most precious non-renewable resource, time.So, the pressure brought about by all the harping, nagging and badgering created a dilemma: Should we carefully and painstakingly organize all of the voluminous material gathered for the book in a concise, logical, orderly progression as originally planned? Or, just dump the contents of the 33-gallon plastic trash bag containing all the cards, letters, paper napkins, torn-off edges of computer paper, matchbook covers and little yellow sticky note papers onto a flat surface and wade into it?We opted for Door Number Two. Why? Because of all the time it would save. We're Sinkies, and as stated earlier, Sinkies LOVE to save time. So, no chapters (this way, you can put it down and take a break any time you feel the need), no organized subject headings, no index, no particular order. It's all here pretty much the way it fell out of the trash bag. Hemingway this isn't.

PREFACE TO THE INTRODUCTION

The original intent for this book was to have it made out of totally-edible substances, and to promote it with the slogan, "Buy it. Read it. Memorize it. Eat it." It required but a minimum of research to discover how impractical that idea was. Now, buying it and reading it are all that's necessary. There's no need for memorization since you're not going to ingest it and render it gone forever. However, if for some reason you find yourself bookless, feel free to purchase another copy, or as many as you like. "Buy all you want. We'll print more." Perhaps you can find a handy spot for your book sinkside. But try to keep it as dry as possible.

INTRODUCTION

If you've ever eaten
over your kitchen sink,
you're not alone
Join the Club!
There are millions of us, many of whom are
members of
**"The International Association of People
Who Dine Over The Kitchen Sink"**

You're a busy, involved, always-on-the-go person who occasionally saves precious minutes by eating while standing over your kitchen sink. Eating food over the sink is a time-honored tradition practiced by young and old. The Sinkie Association celebrates that proud tradition, giving it the respect and recognition it has long deserved. Sinkies aren't restricted by stuffy, old-fashioned rules. They stand boldly over the sink. (Actually, they lean over just a little to avoid crumbs, drips and dribbles.)

BREAKFAST, LUNCH, DINNER OR SNACK TIME! FOOD TIME IS SINKIE TIME!

Many Sinkies are well along in years...70s, 80s,

90s, even 100 and beyond. Sinkieing is not encouraged for those who have not at least attained a 4th or 5th grade education or the equivalent height. A certain worldliness, sophistication and stature are recommended in order for one to fully appreciate the complete, enriching Sinkie experience. The foregoing to the contrary notwithstanding, we know of many youngsters just barely able to rest their chins on the edge of the sink who often engage in the Sinkie lifestyle. We are an equal-opportunity organization.Membership in the Sinkie Association is open to people who eat. All others are ineligible.

RESERVATION NOT REQUIRED

The recognition is instantaneous. Everyone does it. Everyone identifies with it. We all have this one activity in common. It transcends age, sex, nationality, race, religion, economic and social status. And we're all just the tiniest little bit embarrassed about it. (Not like that other thing everyone does and is embarrassed about. Perhaps someday someone will start an association for that.)

There are hundreds of thousands of cookbooks, nutrition books, restaurant guides, kitchen-equipment instruction manuals and the like. This is not a cookbook. There are enough cookbooks. This is a DON'T COOK BOOK. An EAT BOOK. This is a book about eating, not cooking. If some cooking is absolutely necessary, every effort should be made to have someone else do it. Take-out, drive-thru, home-delivered, full-service deli, lunch wagon, street-corner stand and vending machine food are all prepared beforehand and are ready-to-eat. How the Sinkies in those businesses get others to prepare their food for them is not your problem.

When word began to circulate that our Sinkie Association had been formed, it was evident from the hundreds of cards and letters that poured in from all over that people were, indeed, delighted to know of this new opportunity for bonding. Was it a world gone mad? No. It was Sinkies going public. The mail has unleashed a veritable treasure trove of reminiscences, anecdotes, slices of life and tales of tasteful tipping and dripping over sinks from far and near.

Some submissions by Sinkies were slightly edited for brevity, levity or longevity. Naturally, good taste was also way up there on the list of things to consider before going to press. The meaning, spirit and, where applicable, flavor of the submissions have been retained.

If this copy belongs to you, feel free to mark it up in any way you deem appropriate. If doing so helps to enhance your Sinkie dining experience, then by all means, have at it. Underline, circle in red, whatever works for you. This is your book and don't let anyone tell you otherwise. (After you've had your way with it, feel free to BUY ANOTHER COPY.)

You'll note that many of the entries (not entrées) in this book are for the purpose of reassuring Sinkies that they need not feel isolated. This book was written BY Sinkies FOR Sinkies. Take comfort in always knowing YOU'RE NOT ALONE. WE'RE EVERYWHERE.

So, here we go. This book is really now about to begin. Has everyone gone to the bathroom? O.K. If you know of anyone who would be interested in acquiring the movie rights (now THERE'S someone we'd like to get a look at), please contact our kindly publisher. We'll all do lunch.

On the following pages, you'll find: everything you always wanted to know, didn't always want to know, may never have even given a thought to or possibly don't want to know at all, about Sinkies.

THE
OFFICIAL
SINKIES
DON'T COOK BOOK

Legend has it that many hundreds of years ago, well before the invention of what we know today as the sink, the first-known Sinkie was a woman who would do her laundry on a rock just over a stream. This also is said to be the first recorded evidence of stonewashed jeans.

On one particular day, she decided to brown bag it for lunch. She had brought a tangerine from home. She also ate the pomegranate she discovered in the pocket of her chronically-forgetful husband's tunic. "He's such a doofus," she thought as she munched. "At least this time, he remembered to remove his pocket-protector."

That simple, yet unprecedented incident marked the very beginning of the Sinkie way of dining. Thanks to that woman, we are the proud descendants of a heritage that has spanned a multitude of generations.

What a burden has been lifted since I found out that I'm not the only Sinkie in

THE MOTHER OF ALL SINKIES

*the world. All these years of sneaking
meals at the sink and carrying guilt
because I thought it was wrong. I just
assumed it was, because I didn't know
you all were out there, too. Thanks to
your organization, I now feel like I belong
to something decent and respectable.*

LD, New Mexico

Let Us Spray!

Dining while the garbage disposal is on is not recommended. Although not forbidden, the rather intrusive sound it makes detracts from the ambiance being savored and is particularly annoying if you have employed the services of a strolling violinist. (In areas such as Manhattan, Brooklyn and The Bronx, which prohibit disposals, Sinkies need not be concerned with this inconvenience.)

All Sinkie food is Lean (over) Cuisine.

All those famous chefs who are on TV all the time with their own cooking shows; you know who we mean. Sure, they're always preparing some fancy-shmancy culinary creation that rates a 10 on The Unbelievably-Elegant And Overly-Complicated Meter. Then comes all that rhapsodizing about the presentation, garnish and other adornments. If asked, they would no doubt vociferously deny ever eating over the sink. Well naturally, not when they're on television. But, at home... when there's nobody around... we wouldn't be surprised if any one of them was heavily into ketchup-slathered corn dogs right there above the ol' you-know-what.

My husband is one of you people and I always thought he was weird.

CB, Florida

Condiments and salad dressings should be easily-dippable and come in the same type of containers as cottage cheese and sour cream. Have you ever tried to submerge a saltine cracker into the narrow neck of a bottle of ketchup?

As a longtime Sinkie, with a cutting board for a plate, a huge serrated knife for a utensil and junk mail for company, I consider my meals to be a wonderful part of my day.

PL, California

One of the most popular (and exceptionally time-saving) desserts on the Sinkie Bill Of Fare is Banana Lickety Split. Omit the ice cream, chocolate syrup, whipped cream, chopped nuts and cherry. Also, if time is inordinately of the essence, (although we don't recommend going to quite this extreme) leave the banana unpeeled. But do remove that colorful little logo sticker. We're told it's not very digestive tract-friendly.

You have relieved my guilt. I tell you that from the depths of my sink. I know now that I'm not alone.

EB, Pennsylvania

Top 10 Sinkie Unusual Food Favorites

10. Bacon, Lettuce And Potato Sandwich.
9. New England Clam And M & M's Chowder.
8. Three words: Brown Cheese Dressing.
7. Morsels of Fruit Cake.
6. Knish & Chips.
5. Hash Blues.
4. Chicken Breasts With A Side Of Thighs.
3. Mayberry Short Cake.
2. Rack Of Kielbasa.
   And... (drum roll)
1. Oreo Pot Pie.

I cut out a rectangular hole the size of my kitchen sink in the middle of a plastic table cloth. It's very neat, efficient and, in a pinch, can double as a poncho.

GH, New York

**CAKELESS FROSTING:
Eat only the best part. Who's gonna know?**

"Beefsteak Tomato
With Saltshaker Handy."

One of my favorites is chunks of cold meat loaf, preferably made with Dijon mustard, red bell pepper and green onions. Cake frosting is not good for your teeth unless it's cream cheese frosting, to which I plead guilty. Also great: The scrapings from a Pyrex cup in which you've microwaved chopped almonds, garlic and butter (or a suitable low-fat substitute). Another favorite: The garlic bits left under baked, oiled eggplant slices.

MP, California

Sinkies see the glass as half-full. Then, if they drink from the container and the glass remains untouched, they have lost nothing. Some describe this phenomenon as The Power Of Positive Sinkieing.

I eat at the sink lots. I'm retired now and see no reason to set the table just for one person.

GT, California

Helsinki, Finland
Branch office location under consideration.

For a delightful change of pace: Set an elegant table complete with candles (unlit) and flowers (silk or dried). Add soft dinner music from the stereo. Leave this charming setting undisturbed for at least a week while you continue to tap dine. Dust periodically.

NO HOME COOKIN'

One of my favorite dishes is "Sinkie

SINKIES MUST OCCASIONALLY
KEEP UP APPEARANCES

Stew." Of course, it contains everything except the kitchen sink, but has no real flavor unless it's eaten over the you-know-what.

MH, Oklahoma

"Spoona Toona"

My wife is a helpless Sinkie. She will even leave me sitting at the table while she finishes eating at the sink. I no longer think that she has a short circuit or two. Now, I think of her as what she is, a Sinkie. I consider myself a non-Sinkie enabler.

JK, New Jersey

EATING OVER THE SINK: DELICIOUS, NUTRITIOUS, NO DISHES!

For those occasional times when a Sinkie has not even one second to spare: Throw everything into the blender. Press "Liquefy." Press "Off." Voila! It's a Smoothie! Chugalug.

"I'M AT YOUR DISPOSAL."

There must be hundreds of thousands of people who, all their lives, have eaten the majority of their meals while standing at the kitchen sink, yet they remain the silent underclass of the Culinary Establishment. They don't appear in print media advertising, nor are they seen on TV commercials. Public Television cooking shows do not feature a single meal prepared for standing consumption at the kitchen sink. I'm a middle-aged bachelor embarking upon an early retirement. I have a stainless steel double sink, flush-mounted with the disposal on the left. My usual dining position is on the left. Occasionally, a female guest will occupy the right side.

BL, California

(Sinkies who have invited company over to share a meal or snack may put on airs up to and including extending a pinky. But that's it. Sinkies are, by their very nature, unpretentious. They are down-to-earth people. Not highfalutin. Certainly not lowfalutin. Mostly mid-rangefalutin. Sinkies do stand, but not on ceremony.)

We all eat over the sink, at least those of us who can reach.

RB, California

Do you like cold breakfast cereal in root beer? Or a chocolate bar between two pieces of buttered, white bread?

BR, Illinois

Simple Sinkie Utensil Cleanup Method: Rinse and Shake Dry.

When I began eating over the sink, I was just hungry and couldn't wait. Then, it became so practical. Sometimes I eat out of the pot, just leftovers. Saves dishes. I seriously worry at times that I may become table-impaired. Basically, I'm a stand-up person.

LP, North Carolina

When mealtime is brief: "Strawberry Short Cut." Similar to strawberry short-<u>cake</u>, except one of the three ingredients (strawberries, cake or whipped cream) is omitted.

TODAY'S BLUE SINK SPECIAL: THE CONTENTS OF YESTERDAY'S DOGGIE BAG.

Juicy oranges and messy watermelon are especially tasty when no one is watching.

RB, California

Pablum: Rookie Sinkie Food.

To a slow dancer, a "dip" is the highlight, yet most dangerous part, of the dance. To a law enforcement officer, a "dip" is a pick-pocket. To a Sinkie, a "dip" is anything wet or sticky with which anything dry or un-sticky can be joined, if only briefly.

I've been eating as a Sinkie for the past twenty-three years.

FS, Arizona

You'll find no bewildering nutrition claims in this book. We leave that entirely to the Food Packaging Industry, Department of Confusion and Gobbledygook.

I've been a Sinkie for many years. Didn't know there was another way to eat.

ML, California

PRECARIOUSINKIESTACK: One cherry tomato on a dollop of egg salad on a radish slice on a carrot slice on a cucumber slice on a cracker. Not recommended for the dentally unbalanced.

At last! A classification for my addiction! My habit! My thing! Most important of all, credibility and the gift of dignity extended to my preference of where and how to dine. From this day forward, I

shall no longer endure the "jibes" of my husband and children, as I most proudly proclaim membership in Sinkies. Damn the torpedoes, spoons, knives and forks! I'll stand by my choice, and stand by my sink!

JP, Florida

Quick weight-loss trick: For one month, eat nothing but those tempting, mouth-watering color pictures of food from the coupon sections of the Sunday paper. (On second thought, ignore this.)

Feast over faucet! — SINKCLICHÉ

I'm a devout over-the-drain diner and my lady friend is as enthusiastic about this sensible mode of dining as I.

JW, California

Experience has proven that things which rhyme SOUND good to eat, but don't necessarily TASTE that way. For instance: SQUASH NOSH, APPLE SCRAPPLE and ANTELOPE CANTALOUPE. How many more can you think of?

Now I know that my dad and I are not the only ones who do this. He's the one who taught me to eat my breakfast at the sink.

SZ, Michigan

Pig out and clutch some bun!
(Hot Dog, Hot Cross, Whatever)
Everyone should have a roll model!

"Overripe Plum with Paper Towel Accompaniment."

I've lived in shame, hid my addiction from my son and swore the dog to life-long secrecy. I thought I was alone in my sin, but now there's help for us all if we but come out of the cabinet. Thank you for your efforts to eliminate guilt in the world.

KJ, Missouri

Some people spend too much of their lives waiting for things to thaw, jell, marinate and dissolve. Sinkies know how to spend that time more productively.

Insomniac: Sinkie With A Flashlight.

I have a daughter who is a midnight raider of the ice box. The whole family usually leaves doggie bags when she comes to visit.

HV, California

Eligible to become ASSOCIATE members of The International Association of.... er... PEOPLE...Who Dine Over The Kitchen Sink: The Jolly Green Giant, Sprout, Mr. Peanut, Granny Goose, Tony The Tiger, Morris the Cat, Elsie the Cow, Cap'n Crunch, The California Raisins, Poppin' Fresh, Snap and Pop. (We understand Crackle is not much of a joiner.)

Although I love to cook, I'm guilty of eating this way.

JJ, California

Letter from camp:
   Dear Mom,
   Today we had basbal, swiming and trak meet.
   Love, Sonny.

Dear Sonny,
Tell your counselor not to let you have any more trak meet, only brisket.
Love, Mom.

I've eaten many a meal over the sink. For years, I maintained that if I didn't sit down to eat, the food wouldn't stop at my hips. I've eaten many a meal over a hotel bathroom sink. The most memorable was in China, eating Jello with chopsticks. How I learned to eat over the sink? I had a good teacher. My father! He mastered chocolate cake in a glass of milk, and apple pie with gravy!

DS, Texas

DROOL HAPPENS.

I've been a closet Sinkie for many years and was unaware that there were so many other people like myself in America and throughout the world. The cloud of guilt and shame need no longer hang over my kitchen.

SI, Ohio

IMMEDIATE STANDING FOR PARTY OF ONE OR MORE.

Sinkies most often drink directly from the container. That way, the only rinsing necessary is the chin. Sinkies with double-chins are still ahead of the game.

I've been a Sinkie since my law school days. I can recall one of my classmates eating thawed TV dinners directly from the container while standing over the sink. As for me, food preparation means pouring milk into a cereal bowl rather than drinking it directly from the carton. Congratulations on elevating the Sinkie culture to the level it deserves.

MM, California

"Crumbs On Thumbs"
Wet thumbs. Press down on food particles of choice. Lick!
Dessert Variation Of Above: Cookie crumbs on peanut butter on index finger. Lick! (Licker license not required.)

'Tis an ill cook who cannot lick his own fingers.

WS, Stratford-upon-Avon

Sinkies know that a major Halloween trick-or-treat haul can serve as dessert through the following October, sometimes even beyond.

As a Foods Instructor, I'm always in search of different teaching approaches to spark the interest of today's worldly teenager who relishes the unique, no matter what the subject. I know eating at the sink is something my students do at home. Why not include it in class?

SK, Pennsylvania

All Sinkies have gone through Basic Draining.

One cannot eat a decent bacon, tomato and egg sandwich <u>except</u> over the sink.

EW, California

Sinkies never have to endure rude service.

A square meal is not
a handful of Cheez-Its

Fixin's: These are things a meal should always have ALL of. If a meal has only SOME of the fixin's, it needs fixin'.

Anonymousinkie

I read an article about you and never knew what I was until then. Now I know.

ED, Arkansas

**Favorite Sinkie Leftunders:
Popunders and Turnunders**

I'm a confirmed Sinkie and am relieved and encouraged to know that others also suffer from this debilitating syndrome. I have carried sink-dining to the extreme by equipping my kitchen with a sink-side TV and single barstool conveniently

placed at sink height. Occasionally, I dust the cobwebs off my never-used dining table for the sake of appearance. My dining habits are ridiculed by my neighbors, as the sink area is clearly visible to them through the window. My most unforgettable sink dining experience was when I unintentionally inflicted a black eye on myself with the faucet, while eating a head of lettuce. An entire head of lettuce, I might add. "Safety Tips For Sinkies" might be a worthwhile topic for future consideration and discussion. I'd be pleased and honored to provide some input.

BR, California

Safety Tip:
Try not to bump your head on the faucet, be knocked unconscious and drown.

I, too, have eaten many a meal over the sink and find the process to be neat, fast and efficient, right up to the point where the food disposal grabs the end of my tie and I lose consciousness.

MN, Texas

FISH & CHIPS & ALE IN PUB-STYLE SINKSIDE DINING VENUE: "YE OLDE SCARF & SWIG"

Sinkie air travelers are encouraged to continually pester flight attendants for extra packets of nuts, which are, of course, to be taken home for later enjoyment as over-the-sink hors d'oeuvres.

Compared to most airline passengers, who must eat toy food with toy utensils, Sinkies eat like royalty. What's more, they are never required to return anything to its full, upright position.

If you're watching TV while Sinkieing, keep the zapper handy so you can punch out as soon as some objectionable appetite-killer commercial appears. That preparation whachamacallit, for example. Or umpteen flushes. Or any others, *ad nauseam*, you deem "barfo profundi."

"Cereal Dribble" is an over-full bowl of bran flakes and skim milk. The trick is to eat it, do the dishes, talk on the phone and tickle the cat's belly with your foot, all at the same time. The only drawback is that it messes up chins, ties, and shirts.

MM, New York

It is said the expression "Help yourself!" was first uttered by one Sinkie to another.

Top 10 Things Sinkies Rarely Have Time For

10. Anything made in slow-cooker.
9. Anything made in toaster-oven.
8. Anything made in microwave taking more than 6 seconds.
7. Breadsticks longer than 8 inches.
6. Three words: Old-fashioned anything.
5. Blowing on hot soup.
4. Thawing.
3. Unprepared mustard.
2. Small Talk.
   And... (drum roll)
1. Parsley.

I just ate a five-day-old biscuit with cream cheese.

BG, Florida

Suppose for one second a year, everything metal turned to plastic. Millions of tons of refrigerator magnets would come crashing to the floor and make a lot of noise which most Sinkies would find distracting.

Turkey In The Slaw

I just experimented with a nice ripe persimmon, the most plausible of Sinkie creations.

AS, California

In the olden days (Nobody from then is around anymore. We checked.), it was customary for family members to leisurely gather together around the fireplace and share quality time. (Quality time had not yet been invented, but they didn't know that.)

When The Golden Age of Radio came, every living room or parlor got one. The entire family would congregate in front of it and stare at that one bulky piece of furniture. The curtain had opened on the theatre of the mind.

Later, along came Television. The curtain closed. That tiny, flickering screen, encased in an over-sized cabinet, was magic, magnificent and, most of all, magnetic. Mom, Dad, Sally and Billy couldn't seem to tear themselves away. For hours, even before actual programs would come on, the family would blissfully gaze at the intriguing black and white test pattern while listening to an incessant high-pitched tone, usually E-flat. This was something! Boy, this was sure neat!

Fast-forward to today. The 1990s. Busy, busy, busy! Hectic, stressful, do-your-own-thing kind of lifestyle. Each day, the demands on a family's time become greater. Goodbye, family dinner hour! Necessity dictates that the most logical place for family members to meet, albeit briefly, is in the kitchen. And, of course, ground zero is nowhere else but the sink, the nerve center of everything, especially communications. Actually, it's a step or two away, so more the nerve *off*-center.

Today's family members interact by means of scribbled messages on small scraps of note paper underneath decorative magnets stuck to huge refrigerator-freezers whose primary function is just that, a place to place magnetized messages. Some refrigerator-freezers are also used for keeping their contents cold. Once in a while, a Sinkie will encounter another Sinkie, both members of the same family, at the kitchen sink at the same time. This phenomenon is known as Sinkiedipity and affords an ideal opportunity for the two to become reacquainted. The exchanging of snapshots, business cards and carrot sticks can be a nice beginning. It's been said that the family that Sinkies together Sinkies together. Who among us can argue with that?

'SMANGOES (It's Mangoes) Pierce a ripe mango with a fork. Score the skin banana-style. Attack mango at will. Let the juices flow where they may, especially off your elbows.

GS, Wisconsin

25

OPEN MONDAY THROUGH SUNDAY, 6 AM TO 6 AM.

If you can't stand the heat, there's no need to leave the room. Just move a little farther away from the stove and closer to the fridge: What Harry Truman MEANT to say.

I had always realized that I was different. I was a Sinkie. I just didn't happen to have a name for it. My girlfriend did. Slob comes immediately to mind, as does boor, bum, pig, bumpkin, lout, oaf, yahoo, philistine, common, bourgeois, lowbrow and unrefined. I could go on. In spite of all this, my girlfriend loves me and you just know my mother thinks I'm special. Being a Sinkie sounds sane, not to mention dishwasher safe.

LH, Texas

To the few unenlightened Victorians who summarily dismiss or disparage Sinkies as ill-mannered and uncouth, our initial response is a rousing, "Oh, yeah?" followed by "Nyah, nyah, yourself!" and a terse "Neener, neener!" Feeling ever so much better, we then remind our hoity-toity detractors that classic understated elegance, refinement, sophistication, style and graciousness are above the sink of the beholder. Propriety prevents us from pursuing this subject further.

Spaghetti Verticale

One of my favorites is tuna right out of the can. Also, lettuce, celery and carrots dipped in mayo or salad dressing. I eat at the sink most of the time because I can see out my window as I enjoy watching the animals in the woods. I have a bad back so it's more comfy to stand than sit. And eating at the sink just makes for less work. It's easier.

VZ, Massachusetts

Sinkie food is good food. But, is it good FOR you? We don't know. And we say that with confidence.

Gouged Cream Cheese On Thumb

I'm a working single parent with two teenagers who are always on the go. I, too, am extremely busy and always rushing to get somewhere on time. If I'm lucky enough to get dinner, it is usually on the run, over the sink.

SB, California

Proper tooth care would suggest that there should be warning labels on packages of Nuts, Caramels, Peanut Brittle, Bacon Bits, Jawbreakers and Crusty French Bread.

I am a Sinkie of long standing.

VB, Washington

It is said that Former First Lady Nancy relegated Former President Ronald to the White House Sinktum Sinktorum whenever he so much as hinted about needing his jelly bean fix.

At last! I know I'm not alone. For years, I've taken verbal abuse because of my very practical and environmentally

CHEWER DISCRETION ADVISED

sound eating preference. Yes, I'm a
Sinkie. Aside from the obvious time-
saving, we also help conserve our drinking water. Without the need for
dishwashing (and the use of soaps and
detergents), we make a valuable state-
ment for water conservation and protec-
tion. In addition, we prevent the massive
strip mining necessary to extract the
clays, ores and other elements that go
into the making of ceramic plates, cups,
etc. Thanks for your efforts.

MP, Oklahoma

Sinkies are "Over-Eaters Unanimous."

Q. WHAT do THEY CAll A THANKSGiViNG TURKEY
THAT, fRANKly, doESN'T GivE A dAMN?
(BRACE YOURSELf)
A. Cluck GobblE.

Raw Chocolate Chip Cookie Dough
Take a chunk of soft butter, stir in a
bunch of brown sugar, add some choco-
late chips and some nuts. Eat raw by the
spoonful. (Note: "chunk," "bunch" and

"some" are only approximate measurements.)

MW, California

Would you care for something to snack on as you read this? How about a tortilla chip? Also known to serve nicely as a bookmark.

Sinkieing has solved the centuries-old problem of cracker crumbs in bed.

A large mirror, strategically placed, will enable you to watch yourself as you eat, although this is not a particularly pretty sight.

My husband's favorite recipe is Italian bread with barbecue sauce poured over it. Of course, straight from the bottle. No utensils necessary.

CA, Connecticut

A Combination-TV-Remote-Control-Beer-Can-Holder leaves one hand free. Perfect for television-viewing Sinkies (and, of course, couch potatoes).

**FUNDAMENTAL PREREQUISITE
OF THE OFFICIAL SINKIES
QUICK WEIGHT LOSS DIET**

I love eating over the sink by refrigerator-light.

NH, Indiana

Gentlemen-held Lady Fingers/ Lady-held Lady Fingers

We certainly don't recommend that extremely dangerous practice of consuming food or beverage while operating a motor vehicle. Some people refer to foolhardy commuters who eat while behind the wheel as commeaters. Others just call them traffic violations or accidents waiting to happen. We've yet to hear of any Sinkies who have had their dining interrupted by flashing lights and a siren.

I have practiced Sinkie eating Monday through Friday for approximately thirty-four years (breakfast and lunch). It is a very practical, simple way to eat and it works for me. Saturday and Sunday, I sit down.

VP, New Jersey

We all mourn The Unknown Sinkie. He placed

33

pastrami and mayonnaise between two slices of white bread and before he could take a bite, his kitchen exploded. Some say it was a sign from You-Know-Who.

"Power Beanie Weinies." Remove top lid from franks & beans can. Very carefully open bottom lid. Enjoy contents while gradually pushing bottom lid upward until all that delicious nourishment is consumed. Utensils not required.

LK, California

Knish Sans Dish

Pick one microwave dinner of your choice. Follow directions on package for microwaving and prepare when you feel hungry. Use bread from the freezer and butter fresh from the refrigerator. Slap butter onto two pieces of frozen bread and smash together. Pop into microwave after frozen dinner is cooked. When everything is ready, <u>stand over the kitchen sink</u> and eat from container. Plastic forks preferred. When finished,

34

simply throw everything in the trash - no mess, no bother! For dessert, you might enjoy ice cream eaten directly from the carton - any flavor will do.

JG, Hawaii

Q WhAT do you cAll a bickERiNG, baskETbAll-playiNG bROThER who wRiTES whilE hE muNChES oN his food?
(BRACE youRSELf)

A. A quibbliNG, dRibbliNG, scRibbliNG, NibbliNG sibliNG.

I'm only twenty-one years old and already an avid Sinkie. I learned techniques from my father, who is an expert.

CW, Texas

FOOD UNSURPASSED AND UNDUPLICATED. THE ULTIMATE: HAUTE CUISINK

I became a Sinkie when my first child was born thirty-three years ago. What better way to eat tomatoes and chips

loaded with guacamole? Being a Sinkie
also saves on drinking glasses, if you
don't mind getting your hair wet.

JH, California

Have a few extra pounds to lose? Start your own diet and weight-loss program. We call one of ours "Sinkronized Slimming."

Peanut Butter On Apple Slice

I would like to request membership in
your Sinkie club for my husband. Having
eaten cool spaghetti sandwiches over
the sink for twenty years, he is well
qualified.

MS, Florida

Place one pitted olive on each fingertip until all ten fingertips are olive-covered. Eat olives, one at a time, working your way from pinky to thumb to thumb to pinky. Or, thumb to pinky to pinky to thumb. Or, thumb to pinky to thumb to pinky. Or, pinky to thumb to pinky to thumb. There are additional mathematical possibilities which specify index, middle and ring fingers but we don't care to go into any greater detail at this time. If you've begun eating and still have some olives left and the phone rings, let it. It's probably not important. You can always schmooze later.

Citrus Quickie: Dip a spoonful of frozen orange juice out of the can and into a glass of water. Stir briskly for a super-fast refreshing OJ.

JG, California

Many Sinkies use their automatic dishwashers, but only for hiding Christmas presents.

'Maters, Mayo & Light Bread: Lift and eat fast or the mayo will drip into the sink.

LM, South Carolina

Dirty dishes in the sink are not at all conducive to the usually pleasant Sinkie dining experience. However, from time to time, such sacrifices must be made. Fortunately, Sinkies are resilient and generally all-around good sports. That, of course, pertains to the dirty dishes being left by the Sinkie. If, on the other hand, someone else (thoughtless oaf) left them, the don't-get-mad, get-even rule applies. (Are we being sinktimonious?)

Another Sinkie delight: Raw hot dogs eaten at the sink or while leaning against the stove. We have become raw hot dog connoisseurs.

DG, Pennsylvania

Q What do they call the guy in the monastery who's in charge of the Pringles? (Brace yourself)

A. The Chip Monk.

It all started a few months ago when my seven-year-old daughter ate dinner at a friend's home where she stated, "This isn't like dinner at our house. My mom eats over a pot by the stove." My friend hasn't let me hear the end of it. I'm a "domestic engineer" with three small girls. I usually lean on the sink because my kitchen set only holds four, although a folding chair stands next to the fridge for those rare occasions when I sit down to eat. While eating something messy

over the sink, I initiated myself as a true Sinkie. The only good out of this lack of partaking in full-course meals is the eleven pounds I've lost since getting married.

DV, Illinois

Many Sinkies are nutrition and health-conscious. They appreciate having good food without the guilt. LOW FAT IS WHERE IT'S AT.

Midnight is Sinkie Snack Time
before Sinkie Sack Time.

After being a single parent, having to put a meal on the table for the past seven years, then finding no need to set the table, I've been trying to force myself to become a Sinkie. I'm very interested in cake-less frosting. I'm a little overweight, but I love frosted cake. Everyone tells me that cake is so fattening, if I can have my frosting and eat it too, then I will be so happy. I have today ordered a rubber massage mat for my feet while hanging on the side of the

*sink. Also, a bib with a curl at the bottom
so I won't lose the drippings and drop-
pings while changing hands or elbows. I
want to spread the word so others, too,
can know the great freedom of lunch-in-
a-hunch, freedom from washing dishes
and the joy of looking out the kitchen
window watching your neighbors at the
table. Remember, the light in the window
can be the flicker of your candle while
eating fettucine with a Sinkie.*

BP, California

Mid-Air Muffins.

Vertical Victuals: It is said that hot, stretchy, stringy pizza cheese was the inspiration for bungee jumping. (Trade Secret: Sometimes we say "it is said" as a substitute for really knowing the facts about whatever it is it is said about whatever it is. Is that clear?) (Also known as phantom attribution.) (We've got to get out more!)

*I have a girlfriend whose been a Sinkie
for the last twenty years. She feels
over-the-sink is the only way. No big*

cleanup after.

WS, Nebraska

Sinkies swallow almost anything
except their pride. — **Sinkliché**

*I'm a Sinkie for four meals a day. Also
use my sink drain board for a desk. Best
place in the house.*

RS, California

Before he went to that big sauté pan in the sky,
legendary French Master Chef and alleged Sinkie
Auguste Escoffier (1846-1935), upon being in-
formed that his fame was not quite as wide-spread
as that of a young lad by the name of Boyardee,
reportedly remarked, "So, what am I, chopped
pâté?"

*It's about time. So many far-out, radical
groups receive all kinds of publicity,
while middle-of-the-road Sinkie-types go
totally unrecognized.*

HH, Michigan

Many Sinkies tend to lean somewhat to the
conservative side of the spectrum. To some, a dry

41

sweatshirt contest is considered an out-of-control, zany, madcap activity.

Sinkieing is to dining what:
- A. Dixieland is to grand opera.
- B. A bolo tie is to a tuxedo.
- C. Fuzzy dice are to a Rolls-Royce.
- D. Three of the above.

Hunger pangs should be felt and not heard.
— Anonymousinkie

Welsh Belch: An appetite-whetting hors d'oeuvre. Place some chopped radishes and green bell pepper on a raw cabbage leaf. Salt and pepper to taste. Roll or fold leaf. Eat and enjoy. Repeat. Repeat. Repeat.

AL, California

Sinkieing is a practice that is much more pervasive than we know. Statistics are sketchy at best. Most do it behind closed doors. But, every day, more and more Sinkies come out of the pantry.

I don't know why, but everything just seems to taste better over the sink.

Countless well-fed Sinkies

Show us a milk container with lipstick on it and we'll show you a fast-track woman of the '90s. — Anonymousinkie

Top 10 Things Sinkies Only Grudgingly Accept

10. Meal-planning.
9. Unmotorized shopping carts.
8. Anyone else in the checkout line.
7. "TO OPEN - LIFT TAB CAREFULLY"
6. Low heat.
5. Ice cream headaches.
4. Waiting for the hot water to get hot.
3. Waiting for the cold water to get cold.
2. Twist Ties.
   And... (drum roll)
1. Chewing-time.

If my sister isn't eating over the kitchen sink, she's eating over the garbage barrel.

DE, North Carolina

43

"Mocktail" is a term someone came up with for an alcoholic beverage minus the alcohol. A Sinkie never uses the term because it is much too cutesy-poo, thereby placing undue strain on the gag reflex.

(Dr. Henry J. Heimlich was born in 1920. For that Maneuver of the same name, we have Hank to thank. Caution: Never eat or drink so quickly that you'll ever need to use it, even on yourself.)

Tap Dancing Sauerkraut: Hold a few kraut strands under hot or cold water tap. Watch strands (TA-DAH!) rhythmically shimmy and shake. Carefully lift "dancing" sauerkraut to mouth. Eat! (5, 6, 7, 8)

MS, New York

There's at least one Sinkie in everyone's life. Who's yours?

One of our favorites is a very thin cracker topped with mayo, then another cracker, then American cheese, another cracker, mustard, cracker, pickle chip, cracker, Swiss cheese and so on as high

as you like or your mouth can handle.
We call it Cracker Stack.

KH, California

SINKIELORE: He was just barely past his 12th birthday. It was his first time. He was unsure of himself. He was about to embark upon, what was for him, a brand new dining experience. There he stood in the kitchen, leaning over the sink. Thinking that a spoon and fork would suffice for this, his initial Sinkie repast, he uttered the words which would become his trademark, synonymous with him for the rest of his life. (The other phrase, commonly attributed to him, had been, it was later learned, erroneous.) In a quavering voice that betrayed its unmistakably adolescent source, almost-teenaged Henny Youngman said to no one in particular, "Take my knife, please."

And now you know the rest... of the story.

(Sinkcere apologies to Paul Harvey, and, of course, Henny Youngman)

To a Sinkie, dining alfresco
means leaving the kitchen window open.

Some Sinkies inform us that they like to catch up on their correspondence and pay their bills while tap dining. However, a few have noticed that the licking of stamp and envelope glue offers little in the way of flavorful palate-stimulation and no nutritive value whatsoever.

I had no idea other people ate while leaning over the sink. Several times, I've taken a look at myself and have said "Am I a weirdo?" Thank God, I'm not. When I lean over my sink and eat, I can watch the birds and animals in my back yard. It's a simply beautiful scene to look at while having lunch.

AW, Missouri

Sinkworking: Sinkies networking and sharing recipes with one another.

I enjoy the tidbits and extra slices of meat and tomatoes and cheese, etc. that are left on the counter.

MR, Utah

NO RESTRICTIONS APPLY

*I don't dirty dishes or utensils that
require washing, nor do I use materials
that require the destruction of trees or
other parts of our environment. Let's
hear it for more efficient food consumption!*

SR, Florida

Curry In A Hurry

Many Sinkies enjoy curry in a hurry. They mainly like it for two reasons. 1. It's fast. 2. There's something about food that rhymes. Think of curry as a condiment, a dip, a topping, a sauce or a flavoring for meats, vegetables or soups. Making curry from scratch is a major project, ideal for someone, other than yourself, to undertake. Waste no time in finding that person.

Ripe Plum With
Paper Towel Squirt-Swabber

*When I gave birth to my first child
And time for meals became sort of wild
I started eating at the sink
Could get some nourishment in just a
    wink
Everything I needed was so handy*

47

Even my beloved chocolate candy
Now they're all grown and living away
But I eat at the sink to this very day.

RS, California

Sinkies always demonstrate a strong sense of responsibility. They never just let the water run continually. Conservation is a high priority. Sinkies are, by nature, practical, down-to-earth, no-frills people. Rarely do they make a big splash.

I've been a closet Sinkie for most of my life. I remember as a teenager (and even prior to that) I'd sneak downstairs after everyone else was asleep, spread half the contents of our large refrigerator on the counter by the sink (cold meats, salads, breads, spreads, cold vegetables, congealed gravies, etc., etc.) and have a regular feast. Of course, the next day, my dear mother would wonder what happened to all the leftovers she'd planned to use for that day's supper. I must admit I'd much rather eat cold fried chicken, pick on turkey carcasses, eat spoonfuls of anything and everything right out of the little covered re-

frigerator storage containers, and above all, dig ice cream right out of its half-gallon container. Yes, I'd rather serve myself by myself in the solitude of my kitchen on the counter by the sink than dine in the fanciest restaurant in New York.

HT, Georgia

Every single is a Sinkie.
That's almost a given.

Dinner dates among Sinkies are quite common. "Do you come here often?" and "What's your sign?" are rapidly being replaced by, "Sinkie?" (Single Sinkies seemingly speak succinktly.)

Q. WHAT CAN RESULT WHEN A ROMANTIC COUPLE dINES ON SMALL STRIPS OF dRIED POULTRY MEAT?
A. Dinky Sinkie Turkey Jerky Hanky Panky

My son is an artist and his apartment is done in canvas and paint. The only recognizable structure outside his bathroom is his kitchen sink. I consider him

SINGLE SINKIE DATE

to be a Sinkie pioneer, an over-the-sink gourmand of world class.

RH, California

Things one might ponder while chewing:
Is there a Mr. Paul? Mr. Dash? Aunt Ben? Uncle Jemima? Mr. Fields? Papa Celeste? Hungry Jill?

SINKIES GET THINGS DONE IN SHORT ORDER

Finally, at last, we are out of the closet, into the open. No more sneaky looks out the window to see if neighbors are around. No more pretending that only mangoes have to be eaten that way. Everything tastes better over the sink.

WM, Louisiana

Every day, we spend a considerable amount of time over the kitchen sink. Add to that the time we spend over the bathroom sink and it begins to give us cause for concern. Concern escalates to alarm in the case of those of us who also find ourselves above the laundry tray. For those, perhaps there should be a special support group.

Sinkie term of approval: NOW you're not cookin'!

I find myself standing over the sink eating and/or drinking very un-nutritional but very fast whatever-is-closest-to-the-front-shelf-of-fridge-or-cupboard foods. The reason for this development in my life is a beautiful little four-month-old baby daughter that we were blessed with. I also have become very proficient at being a one-handed Sinkie since she generally requires at least one arm for her little self to be held, no matter how hungry Mom gets. So, when I read about your Sinkie group, I truly felt that experience of fellowship, mothership, peopleship, whatever. This letter would have been neatly typed, however, I haven't yet mastered a one-handed typing technique.

MB, California

Eating over the sink is eating on the cheap, and cheap is chic. It costs less to maintain the Sinkie lifestyle. Sinkies know a good value when they see one. And eating one or two quick, economical meals or snacks a day, or a few per week, is one of the most value-packed methods of keeping the old bod well-fueled. Definitely not upscale. Perhaps mid-scale, downscale or off the scale completely. But, no wretched excess here. As dedicated as we are to all that is noble and good about being a Sinkie, even we feel that consuming three meals, plus snacks, per day while standing over the sink is excessive. To those who insist upon doing so, we beseech them to get a life. After all, too much of a good thing is just, well, too much.

Hand-Held Honeydew

A couple of my father's favorite over-the-sink meals: Weiner water over Wonder bread and spotted bananas mushed onto a graham cracker with a Kool-Aid chaser.

TS, Texas

Sinkius Erectus: How archaeologists, 10 million years from now, will probably refer to us.

When I was in college in the '60s, my

*roommates and I doubled our plate use
by removing them from the sink and
eating off the backs. It cut down on
portions, but was worth the savings in
dish soap.*

JS, Oklahoma

We are the International Association of People Who Dine Over the Kitchen Sink. We are the worldwide networking, support group. We bond with other Sinkies everywhere. We are your "Sinkie Link."

*When I sit at the table, I'm either facing
the couch or the china cabinet. But when
I stand at the sink, I can see the bird
feeder with all its beautiful visitors and
the spectacular yellow allamanda vine
growing up the wall. There is just no
comparison. This is not to say that I eat
all my meals standing up. Just the ones
I can get away with!*

MD, Florida

Neatness doesn't count. Expeditiousness does. Most Sinkies are on a first-name basis with at least one dry cleaner.

Sinks are great places to belly-hang.

MB, California

A couple of old bachelors were telling each other about how they first became Sinkies.

"I bought a cook book once, but things didn't work out."

"Too complicated?"

"Right! Every recipe began the same way: 'Take a clean dish,' so that was that."

I find myself always having to eat in a hurry and run out the door like a bolt of lightning.

RW, Pennsylvania

The earliest recorded use in English of the word SINK was in the 15th Century.

I've even had company for cheese and pretzels sink-side.

ER, California

Q.   Every year, which special day do we set aside
     to dribble Hellmann's or Best Foods from our
     burritos?
     (Brace yourself)
A.   Sinko De Mayo.

*I have both sharp and blurred memories
of the wonderful days and nights I've
spent hanging around the sink, looking
to "pick up" anything to satisfy my
desire to eat it before anyone catches
me greasy-handed. I've eaten it ALL,
over the sink; the most bizarre being
frozen bread-stuffing before there were
microwave ovens. Too bad it wasn't on a
stick 'cause it took forever to roll it
around in my mouth 'til it thawed out.
With fondness, I recall the fun I had with
spaghetti finger-sandwiches and tuna-
casserole bars. As a Sinkie, the most
horrendous day in my life was the day
my husband broke the bad news to me.
My beloved sink had to be replaced. I
couldn't bear the thought of parting with
it. Panic set in. What would I do? Where
would I go? The bathroom sink? No. I
refused. The laundry room sink? Much
too far away from the refrigerator.*

Eventually, I came to accept the new stainless steel sink and became quite comfortable with it. I actually grew to like the new sleek look as I decorated it with bagel crumbs and watermelon juice, among other things. Since then, the sink and I have become best friends. Being a full-fledged Sinkie, I do experience uneasy moments from time to time. Example: I have company for dinner and because of my uncontrollable compulsion, have to excuse myself several times during the course of the meal. Unsuspecting guests rarely notice my eye twitching as I back into the kitchen. All alone, I'm free to eat a fragment of anything resembling food as I "hang-ten" over the sink. And let's not forget the challenges. I have perfected a unique recipe for making and eating an entire egg-salad sandwich without the use of the usual trappings of bowl, knives, etc. It may not look like an egg-salad sandwich, but it's undeniably the real thing. I call it "Chicken á la Sink in a Wink." I would be proud to be a member of the club of drips, crumbs, pickers and dribblers, formally known as the Sinkies.

NM, Arizona

Frozen waffle, nice 'n' crunchy, drizzled with syrup. Delicious! It's a Sinkie Wafflesicle. Probably not as good as toasted, but a major time-saver.

Devour defood
and dedrink
over desink!
> Anonymousinkie at a
> Calypso concert

Here's our favorite recipe: Poach and reconstruct calf's head in court bouillon. Serve with herb vinaigrette or rémoulade separately. Garnish with watercress and heart-shaped croutons. Present with silver plate and table-spoons. This version has been in our family for months. It's called "Brain Over The Drain." Enjoy!

> RK, California

(Probably tastes like chicken!)

Acceptable Sinkie attire runs anywhere from none at all to bib to rain slicker. A plastic bib is usually adequate to stay clean and dry. A rubber poncho or canvas tarp are considered by some to be excessive; by others, essential. Sinkies need not wear their best bib and tucker while dining. However, wearing a bib is recommended. Tucker optional. No, but seriously...

One morning, I found myself, mid-way 'twixt the refrigerator and the sink, standing up eating my breakfast. I had become a Sinkie. I decided this wasn't a lot of class so I added a candle for future dining..

LE, Oregon

Some favorite edible utensils: Potato Chips, Carrot Sticks, American Cheese Slices, Pickle Spears, Celery Stalks. Pita (Pocket) Bread is sometimes considered Sinkie carry-on luggage. How many other edible utensils can you think of? There are hundreds.

Cocooning over the sink. Very '90s.

Although acutely aware that there exists a netherworld BENEATH their favorite chomping ground (a world of trash containers, pine and lemon-scented liquids, powdered cleansers, sponge pads, rubber gloves and various and sundry scullery accoutrements), Sinkies don't spend an inordinate amount of time down there. Remarked one, "Once you've seen it, it no longer holds its initial fascination and charm."

Please make my father-in-law a lifetime member. He's a world class-hall-of-fame Sinkie, especially at breakfast. My husband is starting to show the first signs of this as well. It must be an inherited trait. There are no other Sinkies in my family that I know of.

JR, Florida

To a Sinkie, any two or more things chewed and swallowed in unison may by characterized as a casserole.

Chive Turkey with a side order of Trail Mix Du Jour

Between courses, fastidious Sinkies rinse the spoon and shake it dry. (Some say nothing cleans a spoon better than hot running water and a thumb.)

*My childhood memories are inter-
spersed with my mother yelling to us to
"eat it over the sink," especially during
watermelon season. I've never lost the
practice and have directed my family to
all its benefits. It saves washing dishes,
sweeping the floor and wiping off the
counters.*

VS, California

Only after the tightest security measures have been employed and a Sinkie's isolation from others has been guaranteed, is it time for...Sinkie Finger Food! Soup, gravy, mashed potatoes, tapioca pudding, Jello, ice cream, raw cookie dough and frozen yogurt. Who's gonna know? Sinkies give "finger food" a whole new dimension.

*My husband even laminated our kitchen
table to match the countertop.*

KB, Massachusetts

*Bureaucratic Peanut Butter & Jelly
Sandwich: Spread peanut butter on one
side of a slice of bread. Spread jelly in a
similar manner on a second slice. Place*

the two slices together, making certain the peanut butter and the jelly are each on the inside facing one another. Jelly flavor, as well as creamy or chunky peanut butter option to be addressed at some as yet undetermined future date. Prepare in triplicate. Serves three.

GT, California

Sinkies save time.
Gag? Occasionally!
Lollygag? Never!

New Jersey is the home of the best tomato, mayo, white bread, over-the-sink sandwich in the United States, if not the world.

AL, New Jersey

Hard-Boiled Egg With Saltshaker & Pepper Mill Handy

There's only one place to peel a hard-boiled egg. Over the sink! Hard-boiled eggs and egg salad are favorite Sinkie fare. You're at the sink, peeling the eggs anyway, so why leave?

FREE!

SPECIAL SINKIE

GARLIC PRESS

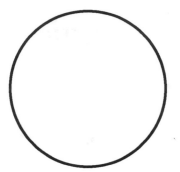

INSTRUCTIONS

1. Place garlic clove here.

2. Close book.
3. Stomp on book.
4. Pry book open.
5. Remove pressed garlic.
6. Buy new book.
7. Repeat steps 1–6.

FREE!

SPECIAL SINKIE

GARLIC PRESS

The person who invented those strong, corrugated potato chips should be honored. So much neater than using your fingers while having a snack. And who wants to dirty a spoon? A tell-tale sign left in the sink for all to see.

KK, California

If you employ a maître d'sink for your kitchen, you're probably at the upper level of upper middle class. Also insufferably pretentious. Same goes for having your Sinkie meal catered.

Regarding our favorite Sinkie...around here he's known as "Weiners Over The Sink."

PG, Wisconsin

Sinkies like to graze at buffets as well as smorgasbords and salad bars. But, their favorite place at which to chow down is their own familiar "Sinkside Café."

For generations, it's been a ritual in my family. It started with Grandpa, "The Scarfer." He used to shuffle back and

forth in the kitchen. Holidays would be his favorite. He'd go from pot to pot. A meatball here, a mushroom there. The artichokes were half their original size once they got to the table. His favorite was cake. He used to leave a knife in the cake box so he wouldn't dirty a utensil. He'd leave the kitchen without having used a dish. All he would leave would be a trail of crumbs in the drain.

Then, Dad. He enjoyed a chunk of salami with a little mustard which he would "wash down" with a handful of potato chips. He also liked cold meat loaf or a leftover chicken cutlet with a smear of mayo. Ask either one of them, "Why are you eating over the sink? Why don't you sit down at the table?" and their answer would invariably be, "Because it goes down faster, that's why!"

KG, New York

I'm very well qualified on this very important art of dining.

JI, Washington

To a Sinkie, tidbit is a food morsel, kabob is a small explosion, kaboom is a big one.

To a Sinkie, as a wonderful finale to an excellent lean-over repast, there's nothing quite like an apple or blueberry turnunder.

Sinknic: As much fun as a picnic, and no ants.

Top 10 Things Sinkies Don't Necessarily Like, But Always Have Time For

10. Fastbreak Breakfast.
9. Fleetmeat.
8. Speedy Spicy 'Sparagus Spears.
7. Provolone Pronto.
6. Swift Swiss Steak.
5. Rapid Sapid. (Stuff that tastes good.) (You could look it up.)
4. Rice In A Trice.
3. Chicken Fat In Nothing Flat.
2. Hot Link Quick As A Wink.
   And... (drum roll)
1. Muscatel Like A Bat Out O'Hell.

You obviously look in kitchen windows.

KK, California

69

Q. WHEN THE SINKIE MONKS AT THE MONASTERY STAND UP FOR BREAKFAST, WHAT'S THEIR FAVORITE CEREAL?
(BRACE YOURSELF)

A. SANCTUARY MUSH.
(Mush In A Rush is the secular variation.)

Enjoy left-overs over the sink. Plates are for wimps.

JR, New Mexico

Cheese Balls are not formal dances in Wisconsin.
- Anonymousinkie

Taqueria: A restaurant for people who eat tacos. Pizzeria: A restaurant for people who eat pizza. Cafeteria: (Pronounced Kaffa-TarEEa) A restaurant where they put beef gravy on your apple crisp. Sinkeria: (Pronounced Sinka-REEa) A restaurant for people who eat over the sink. Why not? An idea whose time has come? Stay tuned.

I do consider myself a Sinkie at times, probably more times than not, actually.

DC, Illinois

There's a Sinkie legend that, when left overnight like wire hangers, little pumpernickel bagels and little chocolate doughnuts multiply.

Food tastes better when vertically-consumed. - Anonymousinkie

I would love information about member-ship for my husband and for my brother, both of whom have lousy wives who rarely cook. My brother was fasci-nated to learn my husband eats many dinners over the sink.

MR, California

Food that's savory, food that's sweet,
Over the sink it's always a treat.

FOR AN OCCASIONAL CHANGE OF PACE, A SINKIE WILL EAT by himself or herself, NOT OVER THE sink, but OVER THE STOVE. THIS GIVES NEW MEANING TO...
THE LONE RANGER.
(FORGOT TO TELL YOU TO bRACE YOURSELF. SORRY!)

A handful of mashed potatoes, no calories. Right?

TJ, Texas

What was the greatest thing
before sliced bread?

*Fellow Sinkies! At last, a society for us!
If you should have a convention, I suggest renting horse troughs - a friendly
way to dine.*

AL, Florida

If you plumb it, they will eat over it.
—Sink of Streams

Fast Food For Thought: Could it be true that you're being recorded when you speak into the sign at the drive-thru and, by means of a diabolically-clever computer, your voiceprints are being instantly matched with all of your personal data and bad people are being dispatched to your home in order to burglarize it knowing you're not there? (Is it nap time already?)

"Sinkie With A Sinker"
(Doughnut & Coffee)

Most of my life, I've been a Sinkie. Early on, however, I had to answer to others around the house. While I'm firmly entrenched now, I would like to offer the following to smooth the way for new Sinkies. There are three sure-fire arguments to justify perpendicular eating habits, especially in the morning where all rookie Sinkies should first begin. (1) The obvious: it's expeditious - nearer the toaster, coffee and cleanup. (2) As you get older, exercises may be performed at the sink - in my case, it's stretching. The doctor said, 'As you age, ligaments tend to shrink, so if you don't want to wear trousers rolled before their time, stretch your lower-leg ligaments.' With elbows on the edge of the sink, I stretch one leg for half-a-toast eating and rest-of-the-toast for the other leg. Equal timing that way, too. (3) Most sinks have nearby windows. While you're eating toast and stretching, become even more efficient by observing nature. I enjoy the

squirrely squirrels, the squabbling birds and their various pecking orders, and my favorite - the slyly-stalking but hopelessly-clumsy young cat. It treads often on rusted leaves on to its seemingly unsuspecting prey. It tries for the kill. However, just in the nick of time, as the saying goes, so go the birds. Of course, true avant-garde Sinkies need no justification for any of their habits. It's just there, the sink. It begs for attention. By the way, eating watermelon is recommended for Tyro-Sinkies.

AM, California

Celery goes with almost anything because it's Nature's most credible edible utensil. Consommé is the exception. Best to stay with cream cheese, egg salad, sticky stuff like that.

Q.   What do some fastidious Sinkies dread most?
A.   Ring around the Kohler.

My eighteen-year-old son is a devoted Sinkie. I was nagging him about his horrible habit. I didn't know this was not

unusual. I've even provided him with paper plates and napkins, but he prefers leaning over the sink. He says it's a great way to eat.

KP, Pennsylvania

In an especially big hurry? Leave the refrigerator door open while you dine. Although not environmentally sound, quite comfortable in hot weather.

Sinkie With A Twinkie

I've been enjoying my meals over the sink for over twenty years.

FH, Ohio

Sticky food is the Sinkie's friend. For example, Peanut Butter comes out of the jar with a knife, but it comes out so much better with an index finger. Peanut Butter, Cream Cheese, Maple Syrup, Egg Salad: THINGS THAT STICK WELL AND DON'T EASILY FALL OFF OTHER THINGS. Sinkie Staples, so to speak.

I've been one for years. Being one goes with being single.

CH, California

DINE WITH A VIEW
OVERLOOKING THE WATER

Been doing it for years. Very convenient. My wife hates it, so every so often I leave her several dirty dishes, etc. Seems to quiet her down for a while. Never eat at the fridge - it's an energy waster. At the sink, I always enjoy the beautiful scenery out the window.

SN, Maine

If you feel entitled to become enshrined in the hallowed, revered Sinkie Hall of Fame; if you're a member and can lean with the legendary, that's good enough for us. As we say, we don't STAND on ceremony.

My father has unknowingly been a Sinkie for the last seventy-six years. My wife also criticizes me for eating over the sink. Genetic imprinting, I guess.

JC, Arkansas

This book is for your kitchen counter, not your coffee table.

Have your own cookout-style Sinkie-Q! Hold a lighted match (flambé) under a savory tidbit on a toothpick. Eat. Next, a marshmallow. Eat. Then, sing a song and tell yourself a ghost story. Variation: Untoasted Marshmallows. Hold unlighted match under marshmallow. Eat. Match may be reused for other recipes or daylight vigils.

The only time the dining room table is given any attention is when it's being dusted, or to leave notes to other members of the family. I have a cake icing recipe designed expressly for Sinkies. The wonderful thing about this icing is that it makes enough to ooze over the sides of the pan. Then it gets almost as hard as fudge, but stays soft enough to be scooped out with a knife. It would make a wonderful finish for a gourmet meal consisting of the last spoonful of tuna left in the can, the last five marinated carrots that never got served and the other half of the small bottle of vegetable juice. I really believe your organi-

zation is worthwhile and will make a contribution to society. When people with like interests gather together, such as those in England who are trying to prevent the removal of bats from churches, the world will be a better place.

ML, Oklahoma

In tough economic times, some people have been known to prepare chicken salad using the recipe which begins, "First, steal a chicken."

I'm a natural born Sinkie. Among my favorites: Strawberries, a carton of sour cream and a box of brown sugar. Dip each berry first into the sour cream, then the brown sugar and you have a dessert fit for royalty. Of course, each dipped berry is eaten at the sink and the stem is plunked into the disposal.

PY, California

Many people have their first Sinkie experience on Thanksgiving night. Several hours after finishing their traditional annual feast, enjoyed while sitting in a comfortably-cushy chair at a festive table with the good china (Oh, did you have to sit at the card table with the kiddies again this year? Sorry!), they head for the sink where they slap together a turkey sandwich constructed in the highest tradition of Dagwood. There, while happily munching, they take the opportunity to reflect on their many blessings and vow to spend more time dining in this newly discovered manner. "Mmffphr Fmumm! Hey, this isn't bad!" they are often heard to exclaim. Thus, another Sinkie is born.

We Sinkies proudly acknowledge that Sinkieing is what we OCCASIONALLY do. However, for Thanksgiving dinner, perhaps this could be characterized as excessive. Then again, a bird in the hand... Or the oven...

For the most part, Sinkies are environmentally correct. No napkins, fewer trees being cut down, nice smug feeling.

I was recently given a copy of a cookbook that was put out in 1938 by a group of university alumnae. Most of the recipes in it are more nostalgic than nutritious, but this one particularly caught my eye. I realize that one of the reasons for the founding of your Sink Eaters group is to eliminate the necessity of the most unpleasant part of meal

preparation; cleaning up. As one who likes to cook and loves to eat, I have searched for a solution without success, especially as I can't get my husband to join me in leaning over the sink. He was raised by a mother who was big on propriety. I thought that you should really have this recipe. It seems ideal, that is, if you can find four or five more people whose arteries can stand it:

CH, Michigan

Studio Steak-A Bohemian Meal — This is delicious-and lots of fun!! For four people, have a T-bone steak 2 1/2 inches thick; for larger numbers, a tenderloin of baby beef is more economical. Trim off all fat and the tail of the T-bone. Rub the meat with garlic. Prepare a paste of cooking salt: put salt in a large mixing bowl and add water until the paste is the consistency of soft snow. Place the meat on the broiler, cover the top with the salt paste to the depth of an inch or more, place under the direct flame for fifteen minutes. Remove the broiler from the oven, take off the salt which will have baked to a hard crust, turn the steak over and apply the paste to the other side in the same manner; sometimes the same salt can be used if the crust is not too hard. At the end of another fifteen minutes, remove the salt and place steak in a skillet in which has been melted 1/2 lb. butter. If the T-bone has been used, cut out the bone. Slice the meat up and down across the grain; the drippings running down into the butter make a delectable gravy. Have a pile of sliced bread, dip a slice into the gravy, put a slice of meat on it and cover with another slice of dipped bread. _Lean over the kitchen sink and eat it out of hand._ Gay rubber aprons can be provided to protect guests. The steak can be preceded by a plain lettuce salad with various hors d'oeuvres, which the guests consume while waiting for the steak. They invariably like to watch the process. An electric oven should be preheated to 500 degrees; when meat is put in, turn off bottom element.

BD, California

(The above gives new meaning to the words, Lean Beef.)

To a Sinkie, ALL MAJOR & minor CREDIT CARDS are UNNECESSARY.

I'd like to share my lunch-munch ideas subtitled "Enjoying Nutritious Frozen Vegetables Without Pot, Pan, Plate or Fork." Especially good in hot weather.

LS, North Carolina

To a Sinkie, a perennial favorite is "Anything Au Gratin": Just shake some shredded or grated cheese on whatever (just your hand will do in a pinch) and enjoy. Mmmm! Tangy!

Scarfing, wolfing, gobbling, munching, mega-masticating, guzzling, swilling are all acceptable methods of Sinkieing. Somewhat unattractive, perhaps, but acceptable.

MEMO TO LIQUID DIETERS WHOSE TURNIP TRUCKS LACK GUARD RAILS: A 47 course, over-the-sink luau is not considered a sensible dinner.

I recently married the most wonderful Sinkie in the world. We've known each other for four years. Prior to meeting him, my best friend drove me nuts eating over the sink. Then, to fall in love with a Sinkie, well, you can imagine my shock.

MB, California

Good Eats: Ambrosia washed down with nectar.

Our Sinkie Think Tank is located at World Headquarters in Santa Rosa, California, USA. Once in a while, we like to refer to it as our Thinkie Sink Tank. That's because we still haven't decided whether Sinkie Think Tank or Thinkie Sink Tank is more fun to say. (Every so often, we find ourselves with just a little too much time on our hands. But not enough to sit down and eat.)

I've been a Sinkie since 1988. My friends all thought I was a bit "tetched" when I'd tell them I just finished my "sink lunch."

MB, Arizona

83

Puttin' (Anything) On The Ritz (cracker, of course).

Just wanted you to know it's about time we Sinkies came out of the closet.

GM, California

It comes as no surprise to learn that suspected Sinkie Orson Welles named his cherished sled, "Tastebud."

My favorite Sinkie meal is steamed crab legs and rhine wine.

MW, Florida

One Sinkie's early recollection: "My mother used to bake all kinds of muffins. After she'd remove those little paper things from their little bottoms, she'd let me scrape the remaining stuff off with my teeth, kind of artichoke-leaf style. But, she said I had to do it over the sink or I'd make a mess. I wonder if orthodontists invest in muffin-paper companies."

Solitude Food
(Greta Garbo was probably a Sinkie).

Over the kitchen sink, I prefer peanut butter and bread or cream cheese and crackers (with pickles and olives respectively). Late at night, my all-time favorite sink snack is peanut butter and bread with green olives or dill pickles and a glass of non-fat milk. (Chocolate cake and dill pickles are also great if you're not counting calories.) Thanksgiving leftovers make great sink fare: Cold sweet potatoes, cranberry-jello salad, cold stuffing with cranberry sauce. Also, pumpkin pie for breakfast is always a winner. And let all the crumbs fall in the sink.

CC, California

Since time immemorial (which was way before last Thursday), "the kitchen sink" has been the metaphor for that which is, or is not, included, or, the one thing that is just too far-fetched to even be considered. *Near*-fetched things are entirely different and subject to a whole other boring explanation. Often, however, they can be found in the refrigerator.

I think people see themselves hunched over the sink, stuffing food in their mouths and hoping no one will observe them. Of course, one of the very positive aspects is that calories consumed above the sink don't count. Thank you for taking a second out of your busy eating schedule to read this.

KW, New York

Top 10 Things A Sinkie Will Not Stand For

10. A sinkful of crud-encrusted dishes.
9. Curds and Whey. No whey!
8. An expiration date on sour cream. Inscrutable!
7. A sinkful of soaking disassembled carburetor parts from a '75 Pinto.
6. Powdered sugar on egg rolls.
5. Salsa on a jelly doughnut.
4. Relish that makes noise.
3. Standing water documented to have been there over a 2-month period.
2. Pork Rinds Flambé.
   And... (drum roll)
1. Head cheese.

I've been standing and eating since before 1941.

CL, Missouri

(Hey, CL, take a load off.)

If you're accustomed to saying grace or offering some sort of prayer over your sink before partaking of your food, here's a suggestion: Speak as you normally would until you get to the very last word. Then, lean way down and put your mouth as close as you can to the drain, and in your deepest, most resonant baritone (you too, lady), say AMEN! Over in the next county, the Roto-Rooter Man will never be quite the same.

Peas Porridge Nine Days Old Is Good!
For testing the garbage disposal.

Sinkie Three-Ring Safety Tip: Just beginning your career as a circus fire eater? What better place to practice?

Sinkies manifest counter-intelligence.

Are Sinkies members of the counter culture?

Would a Sinkie's favorite fruit drink be counter punch?

Are Sinkies who get a great deal of work done within a brief period of time counterproductive?

Do you call a Sinkie who always knows what time it is counterclockwise?

Are these questions beginning to get on your nerves?

Dipstick Baloney: Roll up a piece of lunch meat and plunge it into the mustard and/or mayo jar. Remove, eat and enjoy.

JG, California

Proper dress for a Sinkie runs the gamut. Attire may consist of anything from fully-clothed to merely a bathrobe, underwear or just the altogether. Many Sinkies streak by the kitchen for a quick bite on their way to or from the shower. They think of their sink as a clothing-optional restaurant.

I live alone and become more eligible for this club everyday.

KH, Texas

Sinkies stand (or lean) over the sink. But, they never lurk, skulk or hover. Hovering is for helicopters.

If I eat noisy things over the sink so that I don't disturb others, do I qualify? How about finishing those last few spoonfuls in a dish, rather than throwing them out?

KH, California

Makers of salad dressing and pork sausage who try to have a second career in show business are only kidding themselves. They should just stay in the kitchen where they belong.

Please send the info on your club. What a great holiday gift for my other half who only eats over the sink. This is fantastic!

CS, Illinois

Licorice candy is black. Its counterpart is red. Known as Twisted-Chewy-Weld-Your-Upper-And-

Lower-Jaw-Together Stuff, it comes in lengths of up to fourteen furlongs and can also be used to tow any boat or trailer weighing not in excess of 1.3 tons. In an emergency, red licorice may be used to tie the hands and feet of an intruder until the police arrive. It may also be employed as a substitute if one's bullwhip happens to be in the shop. However, we believe there is no emergency great enough whereby red licorice should be considered edible.

"I say, Sinkie Sommelier! Which wine would you suggest?"
"Chateau Du Faucette. Always appropriate. Shall I decant a box?"

I think I'm living with the original pattern! I first "noticed" this symptom in 1953. I gather that it's not curable. I'm awfully tired of scouring the sink.

AH, California

Recently, a team of geneticists attempted to determine if a Sinkie could be artificially created by utilizing all of the data and technology that currently exists. After exhaustive contemplation, they concluded that, indeed, there is no question but that a Sinkie could have been produced had a child been conceived by Rube Goldberg and Dagwood Bumstead.

SINKIE UNNECESSARY UTTERANCE:
"Check, please!"

I've been a Sinkie for the last forty years. The only time I ever sit down at the table to eat is Easter, Christmas, Thanksgiving or any other time when the mooching relatives visit in hopes of scarfing up a free feed. It makes a lot more sense to stand between the sink and stove and eat from the counter space than to schlep back and forth to the table, to the fridge, to the stove, to the sink, etc. invariably dropping or spilling something on the floor or step-ping on the cat.

AK, Pennsylvania

To a Sinkie, TIPPING is never ALLOWED, or necessary.

My heart skipped several beats when I read about Sinkies. For years, I felt that I was the only person in the world who enjoyed eating watermelon over the sink, and messy stuff like peaches with sugar sprinkled on them, like eating an apple. Please send me information about membership. Will I need a letter from my Congressman? Or a note from my mother or my wife? I eagerly await word.

DL, Colorado

CHEZ GOOD EATS

I was afraid I was the only one in the United States to munch over the sink. A habit, I'm afraid, from my hurried college days and I cannot seem to break it. At times, I actually enjoy hunching over the sink. It saves on crumbs dropping all over. No mess. Just turn on the water and hose everything down.

JL, New Jersey

Because most Sinkieing is done solo behind closed doors, it is rarely accompanied by conversation, especially in person. However, occasional chats on the telephone do take place. A speakerphone is recommended. For the most part, though, Sinkies watch TV, listen to the radio or stereo, read a newspaper, book, the back of the cracker box, whatever. These diversions can add enrichment to the total dining experience. Some Sinkies just think while they partake of their food and/or beverage. Subject matter optional.

Depressed? Don't go to your shrink. Go to your sink!

I recently read that all food eaten over the sink contains no calories.

EF, California

Pop Quiz (Multiple Choice)

If ketchup – a healthful, nutritious vegetable – takes too long coming out of the bottle:

    A. Just shake it more vigorously.
    B. Use a straw.
    C. Did you remove the cap?

My wife and I have been eating over the sink for years and may hold the title for longest over-sink eaters. Fortunately, we have a double sink which allows us to eat together. However, some of the biggest arguments we've had in the past have been over who gets the sink with the garbage disposal.

GG, Oklahoma

(Two adjacent Tandem Sinkies, one right-handed, the other left-handed, should make every effort to stand with their dominant hands to the outside. Two dominant hands to the inside can cause catastrophic culinary collisions.)

Everyone has a sink stopper.
Why doesn't anyone have a sink starter?
Fast Food for Thought.

SINKIES DO IT _____.
(Slogan ideas welcome)

The Official Sinkies Don't Cook Book is going to be a great gift to my 30 year-old bachelor son who, until now, would only make meals that would take three

*minutes, using the microwave oven, of
course.*

LW, California

*BLT, Hold The B And The L Sandwich:
Place a tomato slice between two of
anything. Bread slices are preferable.*

BP, Florida

To a Sinkie, it goes without saying that "presentation" is not way up there on the list of important elements of a meal. However, the way a meal tastes and how readily it can be consumed are of prime importance. In short, some things are a big deal while some other things are of little or no consequence. For example, Rocky Road ice cream right out of the carton is great. Placed over a doily on a dessert dish is redundant. (It is said that only childbirth is more painful than an ice cream headache. Some of us will never know.)

Faster Food is Fast Food brought home and eaten over the sink.

Spice is nice. It's basically stuff that tastes good that you put on other stuff to make the other stuff taste even better. Experimenting with new and unique flavor varieties is simple when you keep a well-stocked spice rack within arm's reach.

The sink is a wonderful place to have breakfast, with the newspaper and coffee on the drain board. Lunch is so no-muss, no-fuss. Who said we have to sit at the table to eat?

OJ, California

Sinkies should always exercise extreme caution while operating a toaster, blender, automatic can opener, microwave oven or any electrical appliance in the vicinity of the sink. That goes for the TV and radio, too.

Before too long, we fully expect a few enterprising supermarket chains to establish "Sinkie Specialties" sections in their stores; perhaps just down the aisle from SPICES, SPONGES and SPAM.

I'm a Sinkie. I sit at the table for supper but I can't remember the last time I sat down for lunch or breakfast. Things I've

enjoyed over the sink: raw cookie dough, a tablespoon of chocolate syrup, a vanilla ice cream soda, orange soda pop and the list goes on and on.

JG, New York

"Meat Loaf In Your Fist" Add salt, pepper, ketchup and mustard to taste. A savory sensation.

It seems that I have finally found a club to which I should belong. I wrote this letter just to the left of my sink while I ate a donut and had some coffee. I was careful not to spill any.

DF, Pennsylvania

"Slosh That Nosh!" When a Sinkie's dining area becomes a tiny bit messy, no problem. Simply turn the faucet on for a second or two and all the evidence of comestibles and potables will immediately disappear down the drain. Easy cleanup is just one of the reasons why "Sinkies never frown while scarfing food down."

Stovies, Trashies, Fridgies, Walkies, Standies: Sinkie Splinter Groups.

ACTOR: "EATING OVER THE SINK IS ALL WELL AND GOOD, but WHAT I REALLY WANT TO do is direct."

I'd like to join your select organization. I'm a flight attendant. Have you given any thought to us? We do with what we have, and it's usually standing in the galley/buffet while our seated passengers scarf down their meals. Over the years, I've been chastised for eating in my own kitchen while standing at my counter or sink. However rude it may appear to others, it is the most expedient way of dining casually. Of course you're aware of this, or else you wouldn't have started this club to begin with.

JA, California

NO SHIRT
NO SHOES
NO PROBLEM

Sinkies are upstanding, scrupulously honest citizens. They would never tear the tag off a mattress or consume any food or beverage after its expiration date. Some of them have even been known to schedule last-minute pre-Midnight snacks in order to beat a deadline.

My son has been eating over the kitchen sink for years. Not every day, but off and on. At first I thought it peculiar, until I tried it one day and it was rather relaxing. One can stare into space, drip one's food, watch the birds, etc., all while eating lunch.

AG, Minnesota

As a happy loner, the sink and a TV tray by an easy chair are my favorite eating spots. Also, I've always been of the belief that free food, i.e. office snacks and birthday cake, contain no calories.

MS, Texas

Q.   WHERE dOES ONE GO fOR MUSTARd wITHdRAWAL THERApy?
     (GET A GRIp)

A.   THE MAyO CliNic.
     (ANd THE GROANERS jUST kEEp ON COMIN')

"PRODUCTS BEST WHEN CONSUMED
BY MIDNIGHT TONIGHT!"

I, too, am a finger-food-gourmet. I love rice, vegies, matzos and a special tomato sauce eaten with the fingers. (Sometimes the fingers are eaten later. Old joke.) I do like to play with my food.

DS, Florida

If you like peanut butter on a cracker but don't care for the peanut butter sticking to the roof of your mouth, turn the cracker upside down. If it's the floor of your mouth you're concerned with, the above procedure also applies, although conversely, of course. The above menu suggestions are known as PB&J ON A Cracker (Variation) and PB&J UNDER A Cracker (Variation) respectively. The variation refers to the J having been omitted from the recipe. (Is it hot in here or is it just you?)

Top 10 Ways to Spot a Closet Sinkie

10. Fidgety demeanor and rapid eye movement when entering a restaurant.
9. Habitually lifts milk container upward, hesitates, then hurriedly sets it back down.
8. Absent-minded fingertip licking.
7. Never zaps away from ketchup commercials.
6. Nervous laughter around flatware.
5. Says reflection in chrome faucet doesn't seem distorted.
4. Offers lame excuse about baby shower when bib discovered in dishtowel drawer.
3. Never forgets hyphens when spelling IN-SINK-ERATOR.
2. Only keeps strong and corrugated (never plain and brittle) potato chips on hand. And... (drum roll):
1. Always last one to go to bed after Thanksgiving dinner.

With the year 2000 breathing down our necks and what with all this talk about how soon there will be 500 television channels to choose from, there should definitely be room for *TSC–The Sinkie Channel*. Imagine millions of Sinkies dining alone while watching a Sinkie on TV dining alone. Okay, so it's not *Masterpiece Theater*.

Fingertip Honeydip

102

SOMEDAY, A 24-HOUR TV NETWORK
OF OUR VERY OWN

At one time in my life, the ambiance of dining was only experienced with the accompaniment of candlelight and cloth napkins. But, one morning, I found myself devouring a bagel with cream cheese while standing you-know-where. I laughed aloud at this new-found freedom. It's fun to realize that no matter what our pretenses may be, we're all pretty much the same.

BH, California

A LIFETIME MEMBERSHIP IN THE SINKIE ASSOCIATION will make a distinctive gift, to yourself, or, someone special in your life. It's unlike anything anywhere. The handsome Lifetime Certificate Of Membership, measures 8 1/2" x 11" on heavy, high-quality diploma paper, printed in blue on an off-white background, highlighted with the attractive red and gold SINKIE logo seal. Please send $4.89 for each Lifetime Certificate Of Membership, check or money order to "SINKIES."

SINKIE World Headquarters
1579 Farmers Lane, #252
Santa Rosa, California USA 95405

Our membership continues to grow. SINKIES are in almost all 50 States and Canada. May we hear from you? We're standing by. We're ALWAYS standing by. However you display your handsome, distinctive Certificate Of Membership - whether you tape it to your wall, post it on your refrigerator or place it in a solid gold frame, everyone will know that you're special. It is said the value and prestige of being a member of The Sinkie Association is impossible to calculate.

If you'd like information on officially-designated Sinkie products such as bibs, aprons, oven mitts, coffee mugs, can openers, cutting boards, scouring pads, sponges, floor mats, fridge magnets, T-shirts, sweat shirts, hats, tote bags, buttons, key rings, bumper stickers, license plate frames or hood ornaments, send a Self-Addressed Stamped Envelope to SINKIE World Headquarters at the above address. Other than this publication, and other officially-designated Sinkie products, there is no Official Sinkie anything. This includes sink, garbage disposal, plumbing company, cleanser, paper towel, grocery chain, fast food franchise company, chef consultant, etiquette consultant or antacid. Sinkies are encouraged to avail themselves of any products or services of their own choosing.

(Hula Hoops, Nehru Jackets, Mood Rings, Pet Rocks, Baby On Board Signs, Cabbage Patch Dolls, Beatniks, Hippies and Yuppies were all widely known in their day. SINKIES HAVE BEEN AROUND FOR HUNDREDS OF YEARS AND WILL

SINKIES UPHOLD A LONG-STANDING CULINARY TRADITION

PROBABLY BE AROUND FOREVER.) [Because Sinkies also care about life beyond their kitchens, a portion of the profits from all officially-designated Sinkie products, including this book, are donated to charitable organizations devoted to the elimination of hunger in the world.]

The dictionary says: "SINK: A stationary basin connected with a drain and usually a water supply for washing and drainage." Perhaps someday it will say "for washing, drainage and eating over." Sinkies are encouraged to call, write and visit their friendly neighborhood dictionary publishers for the noble purpose of pestering them until SINKIE is also included in every edition. Sinkies have introduced a new word into the language. Linguists, please take note. WE WOULD APPRECIATE YOUR INPUT AND FEEDBACK. Some Sinkies have expressed their desire for us to publish a newsletter on a regular basis. In it, we would share Sinkie news, gossip about famous Sinkies (Selebrinkies), updates on favorite recipes and menu ideas, etiquette tips, subsequent slogan suggestions, additional apt anecdotal alliteration and other stuff. One Sinkie even suggested a name for this newsletter: "SINKIEHOOD—A HANDY (TO MOUTHY) EXISTENCE" To which we replied: "We'll have to get back to you on that." In addition, a goodly number of enthusiastic Sinkies have suggested the formation of chapters, the organizing of annual conventions, even taking group vacation cruises. Sinkies know no limits when they choose to be imaginative, even on those occasions when they're not above their beloved sinks.

What you're reading at this moment is Volume I. It's Volume I if, and only if, there will be a Volume II. There will be a Volume II if, and only if, Sinkies send us their ideas to be included in Volume II. Stated another way, this is definitely the only book we'll ever write. Watch for definitely the only book we'll ever write, Volume II. Coming soon! (Maybe.)

We'd sinkcerely like to hear from you. Send us your favorite recipes and creative concoctions, menu ideas, accounts of your experiences over the sink and anything else you feel would be of interest to your fellow Sinkies.

Bon Appétit!
Enjoy Your Meal!
Don't Make A Mess!

If you believe your sink deserves to be awarded a coveted Sinkie Five-Star Rating, write and tell us why. If you can, include a picture of yourself and/ or your sink. Even better, a videotape. If you want materials returned, include appropriate self-addressed envelope with sufficient postage.

To double the value of this book,
read between the lines.

WE'D LIKE TO HEAR FROM YOU!

SINKIE WORLD HEADQUARTERS
1579 FARMERS LANE #252
SANTA ROSA, CALIFORNIA, USA 95405

To order additional copies of The OFFI-
CIAL SINKIES DON'T COOK BOOK, send a
check or money order for $11.95 plus $2.00
shipping and handling to: SINKIES. (Califor-
nians, add 7.5% sales tax.)

SPECIAL SECTION

For Professional
Book Reviewers Only
(Everyone else, no peeking!)

Just for you, our favorite people in the whole wide world, here's our handy, time-saving method for you overworked, no doubt underpaid, exceptionally astute critics to review this book with as little effort as is humanly possible.

We want you to know how very much we truly appreciate your taking precious time out of your busy schedules to do this. Thank you. Oh, thank you, and sinkcere blessings upon you.

If you think...
"I LOVE this book..."

You say:

"*The Official Sinkies Don't Cook Book* has everything INCLUDING the kitchen sink. It's original, unique, witty, delightful, definitely delicious and should be a drainaway best seller. I can't wait for Volume II of this obviously unlimited, totally fascinating subject matter to be published. So tell me where these brilliant ideas have been all this time. But before you do, buy a copy for yourself and copies for everyone you know. It's the essential book for people who eat."

If you think...
"I'm not sure about this book..."

You say:

"The Official Sinkies Don't Cook Book has everything INCLUDING the kitchen sink. It's original, unique, witty, delightful, definitely delicious, and should be a drainaway best seller. I can't wait for Volume II of this obviously unlimited, totally fascinating subject matter to be published. So tell me where these brilliant ideas have been all this time. But before you do, buy a copy for yourself and copies for everyone you know. It's the essential book for people who eat."

If you think...

"I don't exactly LOVE this book. As a matter of fact, this book about sinks stinks and literature has now sunk to an all-time low. This is without question the dumbest book ever published. Furthermore, it is probably the dumbest book that will ever BE published!"

You say:

"The Official Sinkies Don't Cook Book has everything INCLUDING the kitchen sink. It's original, unique, witty, delightful, definitely delicious and should be a drainaway best seller. I can't wait for Volume II of this obviously unlimited, totally fascinating subject matter to be published. So tell me where these brilliant ideas have been all this time. But before you do, buy a copy for yourself and copies for everyone you know. It's the essential book for people who eat."

ACKNOWLEDGMENTS

THE OFFICIAL SINKIES DON'T COOK BOOK, the definitive, quintessential handbook and primer for eating over the sink, is the culmination of the ideas and efforts of many people. We offer our thanks to all of them. Their information and suggestions (well, maybe not ALL of their suggestions), both direct and indirect, were invaluable in the book's progression from the back burner to the front burner to the kitchen counter and ultimately to right there smack-dab over the sink.

To all who helped in any manner and are not named here, we thank you. We are not the ingrates you think we are. We are just sometimes possessed of a sieve-like memory. Please forgive us.

First and foremost, thanks to Bruce Robinson of Desktop Plus in Forestville, California. Editor, counselor, creative wacko and way smarter than Earthlings should have a right to be. If he ever starts his own country, we plan to emigrate.

To illustrator Larry Bulawsky, our favorite inky Sinkie.

To SINKIE Members, present and future.

To those who submitted ideas, whether ultimately included or not. Had they all been included, this book would have had to be re-titled GONE WITH THE WAR AND PEACE and come equipped with four wheels and a pull-strap.

To Kathy A. Talbert, Judi Miller, and Seraphim

Rose Press.

To Mary Coverdale, Lorna Catford, Gary B. Clark, Violet Young, Marlene Fanta Shyer, Ann Bulawsky, Larry Wilde, Mary McBride, Bernie & Maryjo Hamilton-Lee, Solo Dining Authority Marya Charles Alexander, S.C.O.R.E. and The Sonoma County, California Central Library Reference Desk.

To Dave Barry of The Miami Herald, Herb Caen of The San Francisco Chronicle and Mike Nichols of The Fort Worth Star Telegram.

To Entrepreneur Magazine, The Los Angeles Times, The Dayton Daily News, Erma Bombeck and Universal Press Syndicate, The Santa Rosa Sun, Jann Malone and The Richmond Times-Dispatch, Sonoma Style Magazine, Gaye LeBaron, George Hower, Mary Carroll and The Santa Rosa Press Democrat, Paul Harvey and The ABC Radio Network, The Chicago Tribune, John Lehndorff and Knight-Ridder Newspapers, The Washington Post News Service, Sonoma Business Magazine, Ray Orrock and The Alameda Newspaper Group and Susan Deitz-Single File and The Los Angeles Times Syndicate.

To The St. Petersburg Times, Milwaukee Journal, Greensboro News & Record, Las Vegas Review Journal, San Diego Union Tribune, Maui News, Mankato Free Press, Boulder Daily Camera, Columbia State, Buffalo News, Oklahoma City Daily Oklahoman, Torrance Daily Breeze, Covina San Gabrial Valley Daily Tribune, Phoenix Arizona Republic, Syracuse Post Standard, Neptune Asbury Park Press, Oakland Tribune, Ventura Star Free

Press, Bay City Times, Beaver County Times, Southwest Daily News, Topeka Capital-Journal, Arkansas Democrat Gazette, Chicago Sun-Times, Fort Meyers News Press, Lincoln Journal, Lubbock Avalanche-Journal, Atlanta Constitution, Grand Rapids Press, Omaha World Herald, New York Daily News, Chambersburg Public Opinion, Philadelphia Inquirer, Palm Beach Post, Akron Beacon Journal, Sacramento Bee, Sarasota Herald-Tribune, Portland Oregonian, Rapid City Journal, Asheville Citizen-Times, Fort Lauderdale Sun-Sentinel, New York Newsday, and San Jose Mercury News.

To Gary McKee and WSB, Kevin Mathews and WLUP and Brent Farris and KZST.

To all the other print, broadcast and cable media, of which we're innocently unaware or which we may have inexcusably overlooked, who also gave so generously of their space and time.

Lastly, to all the people who make sinks, without whom we would all eat over... never mind... we don't even want to think about it.

Most sinkcerely,

N.H.

My name is

_____

I'm a Sinkie.

Here are some of my favorite
Over -The - Sink culinary concoctions:

BREAKFAST:

LUNCH:

DINNER:

SNACKS:

Culinary Concoctions Continued...

OFFICIAL SINKIE INFOMERCIAL

A Lifetime Membership in the SINKIE Association costs only $4.89. It will make a distinctive gift for yourself or someone special in your life. Our handsome **LIFETIME CERTIFICATE OF MEMBERSHIP,** suitable for framing, measures 8 1/2" x 11" on heavy, high-quality diploma paper, printed in blue on an off-white background, highlighted with an attractive red & gold SINKIE logo seal.

Members are entitled to a 25% discount on any SINKIE products such as bibs, aprons, coffee mugs, cutting boards, magnets <u>and additional copies of *THE OFFICIAL SINKIES DON'T COOK BOOK.*</u>

To order a SINKIE MEMBERSHIP CERTIFICATE or additional copies of *THE OFFICIAL SINKIES DON'T COOK BOOK,* send this order form with a check or money order to:

Sinkies
1579 Farmers Lane, #252
Santa Rosa, California USA 95405

Dear Sinkies:
    Please send me the following:
____ copies of *THE OFFICIAL SINKIES DON'T COOK BOOK*
  @ $11.95 each/ or $8.95 each for members .... $ _____

___ SINKIE LIFETIME CERTIFICATES OF MEMBERSHIP
  @ $4.89 each .... $ _____

SALES TAX (7.5% for California residents) .... $ _____

SHIPPING
  $2.00 per book/$1.00 per certificate .... $ _____

TOTAL ENCLOSED .... $ _____
  Send to:

Name _____

Address _____

City _____ State _____ Zip_____
